*Leap*

## Acknowledgments

Many thanks to the editors of the following, in which some of these poems, or earlier versions, first appeared: *ARTEMISpoetry, Chroma, Dreamcatcher, Lancaster LitFest Anthology 2005, Magma, Mslexia, The North, Rain Dog, Red Pepper, Smiths Knoll, Staple, Templar Anthologies 2006* and *2007*.

'Everything I know about war' won first prize in the Red Pepper / Iraq Occupation Focus Poetry Competition 2004. 'Return' won first prize in the Chroma International Queer Writing Competition 2008. 'The Purpose of Your Visit' was published as a sequence in *Magma*.

'Blame' is part of a sequence commissioned by Derbyshire County Council Cultural and Community Services for Holocaust Memorial Day 2008.

Some poems were previously published in *The Purpose of Your Visit* (Smith/Doorstop) and *You Are Here: Travels of a Derbyshire Poet Laureate* (Derbyshire County Council).

*The Underground Orchestra* (1998) is a documentary directed by Heddy Honigmann.

# *Leap*
## River Wolton

for Terri
a celebration
of poetry

River

Longtodtr
Feb 2011

**Smith/Doorstop Books**

Published 2010 by
Smith/Doorstop Books
The Poetry Business
Bank Street Arts
32-40 Bank Street
Sheffield S1 2DS
www.poetrybusiness.co.uk

ISBN  978-1-906613-23-5

British Library Cataloguing-in-Publication Data.
A catalogue record for this book is available from the
British Library.

Typeset by Utter
Printed by Charlesworth, Wakefield
Cover design by Utter
Cover image: Ophelia #3 by Nicola Jayne Maskrey
Author photo: Steve Dearden

Smith/Doorstop Books is a member of Inpress,
www.inpressbooks.co.uk. Distributed by Central Books Ltd.,
99 Wallis Road, London E9 5LN.

The Poetry Business gratefully acknowledges the help of
Arts Council England.

Supported by
ARTS COUNCIL
ENGLAND

# CONTENTS

*The Purpose of your Visit*

## YOU ARE HERE

The sign points firmly south. Hathersage B6001.
It's wrong. That is the Bakewell road. We glare,
imagine Easter visitors, a Scottish family en route to Derby
frowning, with a quarry wagon at their back,
the primary school about to spill across the lane like sheep.

Should we leave a note
pinned high as we can reach?
Warning. You are not where you seem.

Today we're here. I feel it in the way
we amble through the house,
the path the sun makes on the kitchen floor,
hours like a slowly rolling ball.

I'm down to leeks chopped fine, half-hearted DIY;
your arms slip round me as I wash the pots.
Despite my well-worn maps
we're here, wherever that may be
and here is moving with us as we go.

'On the road out of the woods, we met.'

On the road out of the woods, we met.
She wore a cashmere coat,
a silk-lined hunting hat.

Once home she sat in the best chair
but soon was everywhere –
door handles, envelopes.
She took control of faces.

I got to know her well.
She has twelve kinds of scimitar,
long red gloves,
a shelf of glittering prizes.

Sometimes I find her in my skin,
my hand stuck on a set of cards
with no match
and no letting up.

When we're alone I pace,
or simply stand
because she grasps my feet
until the blood is stopped

and anything
that could have happened next
is augered
with her pointed silver teeth.

## TO THE ISLAND

Fingers prod each syllable
as Janet and John row bravely
from shore.

My shoes are stowed
in a brown bag
by the door.

There's been a drill.
The upper school has clattered
down the fire escape.

They're lined up
on the smooth stretch
of forbidden lawn.

I'm stuck on Is-land.
All she says is *No* and
*Try once more*.

# SORRY

When the first Sorry
took shape
and left her mouth,
it hardly made a mark.

She hadn't put much into it.
*Say Please.* Please.
*Say Sorry.* Sorry.

The second Sorry was larger.
She'd seen how Sorry worked.
It was barely prompted:
*Look what you've done.*

She cut a sliver of herself
to offer with the word
and buy her peace.

But Sorry whittled her away
until she was a hollow girl
with an out-of-date coin
on her tongue.

## NOTE TO SELF

Not hate, more like wanting to sting you awake,
fling a basket of midges like the mistakes
you try to forget. I'm sending you pinches at dawn
and a bruise in the chest to remind you
each time you draw breath. All you need do
is behave like a well-ordered woman
in Regency dress dancing a Pavanne. Look,
I'm sending you steps that are easy to copy.
Move on. Here are nails bitten down,
a knife and a lemon, the yelp of the days
yet to come, that demand you inhabit them.
Pull them towards you hard, like a hand on a gun.

# REPUBLIC OF SLEEP

Alarm slapped off, you're pinned to the pillow
till you tip out, slump towards the shower.
The after-breakfast lull tempts you
while traffic climbs the hill and crisp commuters frown.

Inertia silts the desk, leaks into afternoons
that should be punctuated with the keyboard's click,
entices you from deadlines, friends whose company
you know you want to keep. Sleep bars the door,

establishes frontiers, commands you to lie down.
No more the nanny lulling your drowsy pram
beneath a cherry tree, it hands you to the guards
who have no use for you or for the life you planned.

# ON DAYS LIKE THESE

we lay across each other on a giant bed
under a circus tent of a mosquito net,
waking at dusk to ride the highway
to the last town in the world.

In palm-roofed cafés we devoured cornbread,
barely unlinking hands to lift our forks.
The only place on earth where smiling waiters
ask two women *Are you newly wed?*

Nurse-sharks beneath the jetty beams,
ants peppering the sheets, all were beloved.
Even mosquitoes, finding each tear in the fabric,
we gently pushed them out

with the large-heartedness of whales;
as though we'd turned amphibious,
dragging our bellies through coral or lagoon
opening and closing our huge mouths.

# THRILL

The second time we met we drove inland,
launched the hired canoe into the Everglades,
mosquitoes' needle-hum. Mid-afternoon
and still the sun pierced through my hat.

We were too far from shore when the alligator
leapt and smashed down to the surface.
We'd seen a seven-footer stalk between the tents;
dogs, a Ranger told us, are the usual accidents.

Five, ten, arched their bellies to the sky.
Water narrowing, we reined the paddles in
and, head-on, a green snout V-ed the lake's skin,
diving as it paralleled the boat.

In each encounter there's a snapshot of the years to come.
For us it was this darkened undertow
that sensed us well but didn't change its course
while our hands bristled for each other.

As we hauled ourselves through rising mud –
that we'd been warned not to approach – the thrill:
of comradeship, of proving all the voices wrong,
and ridges of relentless hidden teeth.

## WHAT YOU DID

Said Yes. Dived with her from the old road-bridge.
Ploughed the current to the mangrove island.
Scooped snapper from the ocean with bare hands.
Roasted it on driftwood over flames coaxed
from dead leaves and combed-out hair. Spoke
even when your tongue froze in your throat. Stayed
while the sun dripped from the sky. Beat back
immune to shark or barracuda hanging
underneath the waves' green lip. Split
moon-edged water no match for your biceps
and trapezius honed since youth, cultivated
over years in gyms: your upper-body strength.
The lack of which makes all of this a lie.

## SIERRA NEVADA

Classic mistakes:
set out too late,
wore flimsy shirts.

We stripped,
dawdled in a lake,
ignored the sun's descent.

You loved it from the start.
I sobbed, predicted frost –
autumn, near Spain's highest peak.

Dark unleashed our common sense:
we stockpiled kindling,
dug matches and an orange from the pack.

Vanity dissolved. I wore two hats,
buttoned everything, acquired burrs
that still cling to those socks.

You slept like a stone.
This was our highlight:
night vision, silence.

# RECONCILIATION

There's a blue-black crow beating her head on the glass,
gleaming beak against her own reflection; all I know
is we go forward with our fists raised and meet ourselves.
No, that isn't what I know, I read it in a book.
All I know is that at three-thirty a.m. I looked at you
and all the things in which I recognised myself,
purple scarves, black knickers, a dog-eared filofax,
the things that had my name on them,
that I loved and missed even before I lost them,
the certificates, the photographs of holidays
with dates and times, witnessing that I was there
walking the earth, in my size thirty-nine-and-a-halfs,
the right foot slightly heavier than the left,
they didn't matter anymore. Not that I was less
or that I should hit myself in the tender part
of my head and say *sorry sorry* like I wanted your tread
on my neck. All I know is that they fell away
like ballast on a balloon flight, like the first step
weightless and exultant into air.

# GOLD

You thought you had a solid world
in the bed of your true love's palm,
her back beneath your arm,
her skin under a ribbed grey shirt.
The nights she sprang awake
from dreams of rising water;
only you could soothe her;
you thought you had it.
Fever and tongue. Honest and bone.
Hook. Line. Sinker.

Now in the land beyond the love of your life
some days bring relief like the first cigarette
in the quad, the break, the green-pink evening.
You hadn't expected it to feel like this.
That you could want something.
Each friendly glance a lure
ready to haul you to a world
you know no longer waits, that has forsaken you.
That you forsook.

It's hard to stay agnostic, not lay yourself down,
bring frankincense, gold, myrrh.
These days you're drawn to anyone with faith.
St Aidan's United Reform. Rabbis for Peace.
Women with veils. Anyone
whose steadfastness rubs off.
No mantras left.
You think of taking up smoking again
but even that old god is good and dead.

## THE WAY WE'VE GROWN APART

is like my hamster,
birthday present from the pet shop.
I fed him cornflakes, held him in my lap,
but soon forgot to pick him up
and, wary of human touch, he bit.

The way we hardly speak
is like the name my parents gave him.
Omar Khayyam.
Wanting to be good
I went along with it.

The way it carries on
is like the silence when Dad said
Omar had gone to sleep.
And no, I couldn't see him,
there was nothing left.

## WHEN SHE RAN

When she ran all the way from home
to St John St Michael and All Angels
that April Sunday in her surplice
with her shoes half-laced
her parents fast asleep
her bright blue cassock flapping
her head full of *Morning Has Broken*
and the boy who stood behind her in the choir
whose name she'd written in her hymn book
and who'd taught her to say *Balls*
past The Duke of Kendal, Albion Electrics
and The Chocolate Box
she did not know that she was late
that the pews were full
that she would stand at the door
watching the other choristers
processing to the altar
she did not know her parents
could forget to put the clocks forward
did not see their lives slip by
the route she'd take past the vicarage
for Paddington Station and university
she did not see herself at twenty-four
wondering if the church hall
would do for her mum's funeral
she did not see herself turning her back
knowing none of this
was the right time or place.

# LONDON BOMB 1975

Though the windows were gone
though Mum wasn't dead
though flickering tape sealed the street
and post-boxes shrank to a slit

though Dad knelt in the road
to peer under the car
I never imagined us
on any side of a fight.

Never imagined you walking to school
in Belfast, and a brother in uniform
taking it out on you
night after night.

## SUMMER '76

and you're sandwiched
in the sweaty back seat
singing *Waterloo*
along the road out of the city.

For hours you splay
in your school-black Speedo
by the swimming pool of someone
no one seems to know.

Bedtime and your back crackles
against the nylon nightie.
You don't want to take it off
can't stand to see your body,

have spent hours at the mirror
trying to smooth your chest,
exorcise the bumps that swell
through vests like two fat zits.

Nothing lifts the heat.
Your mother remembers
the medicine cupboard, pulls out
Germolene with rusty corners.

In the dark you let her rub cream
on your shoulders. It stains, stings,
and no sleep comes that night
to ease your skin.

# DRIVING TO ALDEBURGH

No sleep makes this sea-town flash blue and white –
another mystery popping from the all-night drive
like Father Xmas in his Tesco petrol booth
who pointed out the way to Felixstowe at dawn.

Roads have peeled off my usual take on things,
all seem to need translation: King Street,
half a pound of skate, leek soup.
Without my well-slept self

there's room for curiosity –
a winter bee lands on the page,
a black-backed gull looks just like Churchill.
Where am I? Gulf of Mexico

or Greystones Beach where Adam and I took all day
to dam and alter the entire course of a stream
shifting our body-weight in sand
with two red plastic spades.

Thank you for not coming back
to check we were still there,
for leaving to track down another 13th Century church
while we dug through to the water table.

# ARCHITECTURE

I regret that I drove her to the Royal Marsden with a case of Evian,
the New Statesman, Yves Saint Laurent hand-cream,
a green silk nightie, daffodils for Mother's Day,
postcards from the V & A, and through it all said nothing.

What if I'd built a bridge, a copy of Brunel's at Iron Gorge –
the one she detoured hours to see that car-sick holiday –
if I'd made blueprints, concrete footings
deep into the water, aimed a steel arch.

I spoke once, near the end, over a jigsaw –
five-hundred pieces of Venetian Canaletto –
*How will I cope?* and she sat beside me,
rubbing my back in small firm circles like a child.

## FEDORA

He's been telling that story again.
The one where he gets thrown out
of the Marlborough Club in 1926
for wearing a fedora and not a bowler.

I don't know what any of it means.
Where his hat was, a freckled dome now shines
with lank grey strands on which I practise plaiting
while he dozes.

## SEYMOUR BATHS

Municipal brown walls. Chlorine's bite.
Like him I'm bony, lips blue however hard I swim.
Afterwards there'll be gritty hot chocolate, salt and vinegar.

At the shallow end, my friend points:
*Have you seen that old tramp sleeping on the benches?*
He's put his feet up; always tired. He's seventy.

I don't know him.

# DOUBLE PNEUMONIA

It's 4.30 a.m. I kneel on the rug
beside the mattress bought to counter bedsores.
*There are blackberries on the wall* you say,
mistaking the Boukhara tapestry.
I wet your peeling mouth. We're a muddle
of centuries. *Blackberries* again, as if the hills
of Edwardian Berkshire are opening
their autumn arms. Your breath stops.
Have I said everything? Minutes pass.
You rattle back into gear like those first cars
you drove, headed by a man waving a flag.
You wake up, ask for Guinness, live another year.

# SHEFFIELD – ST PANCRAS

This is my ninetieth bisection of the Midlands.
Here is the Buffet Bar, its red formica top
over which I've leaned to indicate my choice of Kit Kat,
plastic-coated Dundee slice, free-range egg and cress
or Typhoo, which has by turns been complimentary
or one pound fifty-three. Six swans are gliding
on the burst skin of the Derwent, Liam who's four
is launching paratroop attacks throughout the Quiet Zone.

There's only ever been one train, my train.
This is the same engine that sent me north
and pulls me back for sickness, love
and obligation. This is the on-board payphone
where I called Helen to say my Dad had died
and that I'd leapt into a taxi, hurtled through the station.

This is the seat I curled up in, facing the direction
of travel, this is the stowaway grey table
with its one receding eye where I have lodged my tea
and where I write now, next to my reflection.

## THE UNDERGROUND ORCHESTRA

Tuesday's the funeral and we who've barely
touched since childhood, meander arm-in-arm
along the kindly Thames. The film's about
Parisian refugees – buskers and pianists,
a string quartet who only play for love.
We are ecstatic; it's the best you've ever seen,
I want to dance. Is this what happens
now we're parentless, empty of reference points?
We wander back on streets we've searched
for years. You ponder stacked CDs
for the cremation, choose the perfect Nocturne
and a Bach Allegro like the footsteps
of a small boy running through a room.
I leave you to it, trusting you this time.

# ASHES

Half of him is in a carrier-bag above the gardening books.
The rest is in the tide, a herring gull's stomach,
or slapped onto the keel of a Brixham trawler.
He's in amongst the whiting as they make for Margate,
dotted on snap-shots of Foster's foot-bridge
strung between St Paul's and the new Tate.

We launched him in a cardboard boat, without permission,
headlong into choppy waves. March gusts whirled
the fine grit under my collar, up my nose. I sneezed
and brushed my coat. Too close, as when, adrift and frail
he thought I was my mother, pulling back the sheet
*Aren't you coming to bed now? Aren't you getting in?*

Below, the Northern Line chuntered to London Bridge
as he'd done every day for forty years. He'd have liked
the gallery café, sniffed at the Rothko retrospective,
travelled sedately in the lift. Then, leaning on my arm
with raised stick heralding the way, we'd have wandered
through the installation in the Turbine Room –

a vast sun caught in its descent, a mirrored ceiling
under which hundreds of people lay in stars or clumps
waving at their reflections through the dust.

# TRUE AGES

To the Commonside Rajput with walking sticks,
elbow patches peeling from his brown tweed suit,
ten years a widower. We sit beside the window
of the empty restaurant. He orders Vindaloo
and I'm fifteen again, Sundays at the New Delhi,
poppadums snapping between his wrinkled hands.
*Inside, I still feel twenty-one*, he says.
A waiter deals oval dishes. *Pilau Rice?*
The century warps as saffron splatters –
suddenly I could be ninety with a taste for fire,
an appetite for journeys north, and he's thirty
scribbling his novel in a Paris attic
or gliding over parquet floors with a tall stranger,
holding her cool green waist as time hangs in the air.

## LEAP

There's an emerald lawn below the window
and it's May, which it wasn't when you went to sleep.
A warden in green twill explains they're moving south
and it's his job to tend them. You're surprised,
you'd heard only *Northumberland* on Radio Four
and *isolated clusters in The Lakes*.

They've got this far by following the trees
– fewer, here – and springing over dual carriageways,
but he points out lethal whirlpools
under supermarket moats and as you watch
a Wal-Mart blossoms on the B6133.

She's the blood side of red, all set to jump.
To her you're just a dodgy kind of willow,
but you're so glad to see her
that you lock the foxes in the pantry.

Two have been sighted, strikingly fat and fast –
a sub-species that terrifies the greys.
You want to tell somebody but your friends don't get it
and you're waking up. You glimpse her
airborne, fiery through the glass.

# AUGUST

*On 7th August 1735, six women 'not incommoded*
*by clothes or modesty' ran three laps around Moorfield, Derby.*
*They earned a Holland smock and half a guinea.*

Mill girls, the six of us, cheeks and arms
fired by the dust and the roar of machines.
Betty began it, a lass who'd blush at the drop of a hat.
Her dare parted the smother like Moses.

A day when you want to lie down in a pond,
hold your face to a flagstone,
be resurrected by breeze. The press of sweat
like rogue hands in the night.

Who wouldn't have wanted to run for their life
from itchy stockings, underskirts bleached in the sun,
darned heavy as blisters. The pinch of slips,
stays, bodices, aprons – gone

and as if we'd discovered an island without any name,
our clothes in grey heaps like washing left out in the rain
we plunged right into the holy-once-only.

The smock was to cover us up, and the money – a sop.
As if we'd be caught with a price on our skins.

## MARIN COUNTY

The day after ten days of silence
I came on a king snake coiled in a socket of earth.

A mattress of no words
behind me.

Knowing nothing, I lifted my arms.
My toes stopped just short of his skin.

Sweetheart, I said
and stepped to the side.

A sliver of ink
licked the air.

# MISANTHROPHILE

I hate people because they sneeze, demand
that plain instructions are repeated, die,
and have good times from which I am excluded.
I hate their lack of tails, their taking fright,
their need to whistle and to let doors bang,
to eat popcorn, and sweat while they're asleep.
I hate people because they set exams,
deport children, choose silly names for sweets.
I love them most for their ability
to speak Italian, laugh at pantomime,
invent salsa and cake; and for their knees.
I love people because their bottom-line
is wanting light and fuel, and in that way
they're just like kittens, lambs and baby snakes.

## TO TEETH

Champions of spit and speech! Prophets
of tummy ache as curry, chips and chocolate cake
demand a gangway. I apologise. Nights
I slumped asleep ignoring you; days
I cancelled trips to Mr Moffatt and the pure sun
of his tip-back light. Now that bits of you
are breaking off I'm even missing our farewell scenes
as I down you inadvertently with muesli
or the brute edge of baguette.
Are you still there, holed up in my gut
or shat out, dear ones, no more nibbling
a lover's arm or zinging with a misplaced bite
of Real Vanilla, but at the wrong end,
exiled from roots and sailing out to sea.

## HEROES

Forgive the way they wear their underpants,
their glee at cryptic clues. Remember
that they have a lonely life
and weaknesses –
often something you would least expect:
a yen for apple pie,
an inability to tell their left from right.
Like ours, their fillings glint in certain lights.
They will do anything for love.

# AT THE GYM

I knew it was her from the piercings –
earlobes stretched into loops.
And from her name badge:
Kwan Yin. Welcome to Virgin.

I'd like a Ladies' Swim and Steam, I said
trying not to stare
at the Buddha of Compassion
who hears the cries of the world.

Behind me someone coughed
and shunted their holdall
into the back of my knees.
I wanted to ask

Does it hurt?
Her ears so full of emptiness
I could see right through them
to the snack machines.

# IT'S EVERYTHING YOU WANT FROM THE END OF FINALS

Sunny. The ice-cream shop's open.
You've written ten three-hour papers in five days,
skirting the topic of medieval torture
in a question on the Albigensian heresies.
You've not called for a yard of ale. Someone's
killed themself. You've knotted page to page
with lengths of string draped on the desk
by invigilators strolling up and down.
Now you're going to shove 10p's in fruit machines
and drink until you're in a Brixton attic,
the anarchists next door are Stopping the City
and shitting in the garden, and as you come round
from the Special Brew a German punk called Tina
mutters Why, oh Why.

# DYING WELL, AN EXPERIMENT

We hope the class will learn by observation.
Find evidence: the one who lay above her grave
with open eyes and named the trees for the last time,
left the house itemised; one who soloed gritstone
at midsummer dawn in the full tilt of new love
and lost her footing; one who soothed her sons
in the sealed darkness of a ship she'd paid
to carry them to freedom. No foolproof method, then,
for cracking open like a pale-blue robin's egg,
for taking leave of air and hands and water.

## BLAME

was a seed that fell into our hungry nights,
limbs drained of heat until our pulses beat
only with hate. Our bodies hammered thin,
our children dull-eyed from the lack of work.

It took root as the strangers multiplied,
favoured by tricks we had no way to learn.
Behind closed doors we heard the scrape
of plates, coins, laughter, tuneless songs.

Nowhere to turn, we shrank as blame spread out,
held us against the wall, made us obey.
To put them in their place. To let them know
exactly how we felt. Small. Afraid.

# EVERYTHING I KNOW ABOUT WAR

I see in Shairah's face as she arrives
and kisses me one two three four five times,
this cheek, then that. *Salaam Aleikum. How are you?*
*I'm fine.* Wrenched to this winter, widowed after two
decades of invasion, she gets here early
for the food – white bread, tomatoes, chilli,
cheese, digestives, supermarket hummus,
or home-made halva, pistachios and spices,
a plate of Burmese noodles. Everything
I know is in the faces of these women
even when they smile, in their generosity,
in places language cannot reach. I see
fragments of their houses under fire
from bombers launched in Gloucestershire
above conservatories where people sip Darjeeling
out of willow-patterned china. Everything
I know about war, I know from the silence
after Marie cries *J'ai pas la force*,
*J'ai pas le courage*, when the lawyer's letter
says she has no grounds to stay and must prepare
for deportation. Everything I know, I know
from sitting here with bags of baby-clothes,
from the Rwandan teenager who's too shy
to speak, from the corner where Shareem prays
white-lipped in Ramadan for the Home Office
to relent, for a letter or a half-promise.
Everything I know, I know from the survivors,
*Our lives are over, it's the children now who matter.*

No, there's no official war in Yemen, just three guns
for every person, there's no war in Afghanistan,
no war in Algeria, no war in Congo,
but on the battleground of female bodies. No,
there's no war in Iraq, no war in Iran
where Azar has fled the politician-
husband who disabled her, but since gender
is not *race, religion, nationality, member-*
*ship of a particular social group, or a political*
*opinion*, she does not fit the bill.
Together we push war towards the edges,
for two hours drink tea in twenty languages,
distract the kids. But nothing rinses off
the memories – Suleika's daughters locked
inside the engine-box because the man
she paid to bring them here insisted that
they had to be silent or die. Everything I know remains when almost everyone has left and Jedira who's eight
with butterflies face-painted on her cheeks, says
*Can I stay, can I stay please and sweep the floor?*

# WITNESS

6.45 a.m. A parked white Transit
is not Immigration. Abdul answers the door.
*Everyone's asleep.* I tuck myself into the couch,
wonder how we'll stall the dawn.

In Nazaneen and Sahar's Christmas cards
Byron Wood Primary has said farewell.
Sataish's new toy-kitchen back in the box,
no food bought since last week.

We wait. Should get a removal date,
flight-time but no-one's sure.
The MP says *Go quietly.* Nothing
since last week when they came at 8.

The First Line buses ricochet
down Burngreave Road. Microwave pings open.
Shukriya brings spiced tea and almonds.
UK. This year, this week. So far, so good. .

# SABIR

As I write, Sabir is trying to get here
climbing onto a pitching boat with a
terrified child in his grip and another one
left behind, stepping over the waves
into the tilting curve of the wood;
he is out on a sudden north-easter,
the tide pulling him further, while
he loosens the dark from a corner
and scrambles ashore as a border-guard
looks for the trigger. I hear that he waits
inside steel for a lip-service interview
and a No that is clearly translated.
At the same time his previous name
is in flames along with his birth certificate
which now is commanded as proof
by a summons to stand
before law and mahogany benches.
Simultaneously, he is twenty-seven days old
with a fine head of hair and long feet,
he is under the average weight, sleeps
in a warm orange room on a Tigger rug
under embroidery of the black rock
at Mecca and I am persuading
his mother to eat more than Weetabix.
Everything else is pooled at the gate
like something that happened
to somebody else, which it did,
but it rustles and shakes
as I walk up the path, into the English
autumn light and the warning glare
of a search-vessel out on the water.

*The Purpose of your Visit*

# OLD CITY

Thin cats stalk the back streets
of the Christian Quarter
for fish skeletons and yoghurt globs.

Hot thick air leans in,
graffitied buildings close over my head.

In the Muslim Quarter, half-size tractors
climb the marble steps beside embroidery stalls
with trailer-loads of building blocks and rice.

I slither down, catch a glimpse of t-shirt slogans:
*I got stoned in* (tick-box) *Bethlehem, Ramallah, Hebron.*

Two Hasidim stride by, black coats, Dickens top hats.
One hawks and spits, saliva landing
on the piled fruit outside an Arab shop.

The owner doesn't see or if he does is silent.
I push past, way out of my depth.

# ETIQUETTE

Lisa, a Californian who's cantor in her local synagogue
and volunteers as paramedic in the occupied West Bank,
explains the etiquette of checkpoints:

how the ambulance waits to be ushered forward,
even with patients on the point of death
at all costs don't move first.

One night she spent an hour edging towards
a silent jeep, tapping, then banging on the hood
while the boy inside lay by his gun, asleep.

# STATISTICS

Between September 2000 and October 2004
at Israeli army checkpoints
sixty-one women delivered babies,
thirty-six of them stillborn.

Below the skin of the numbers
stretch yourself into memory or imagination
and see yourself blockaded, labouring,
able neither to go back nor forward.

A subtler poet would work in a biblical allusion
tie a knot with Herod,
with the deadly twins
of history and religion.

I only want forceps to midwife sense,
a scalpel to dissect, lay wide the fear
that keeps an eighteen-year-old's rifle
aiming steadily into the ambulance.

# THE VISIT

I slip through a gate
in Mas'ha, Salfit region, West Bank,
up the stairs and into Hani and Munira's house;
built with full permit, it cannot easily be bulldozed.
Refugees from '48, this time they will not leave.

The single-storey building is enclosed
on one side by an eight-metre concrete wall,
a military road, and on three others
by a metal fence and razor wire.
It's tapped, an armed Settler appears,
and shortly afterwards, an army jeep.

Twenty of us perch on dusty beds.
We meet the family, eat grapes and pretzels,
drink warm Coke, take pictures from inside.
From here you see the wall half-painted
with a child's view of hills and trees.

They let us out through the gate.
A donkey stands, grey, white,
tied to the fence.

# DEPARTURES 4.30 A.M.

What was the purpose of your visit to Israel?
Where did you stay? Did you stay there all the time?
Do you have any friends or family here? Did you come alone?
Did you visit any private houses? What is your profession?

Wait here while I get my supervisor. When did you arrive?
That's a long time to stay in one place. Did you visit anyone?
Who did you meet at the hotel?  What are their names?
What did you do when you were here?

What did you do yesterday, for example?
Did you go anywhere outside the Old City?
Where do you live in England? Are you getting a direct flight?
Do you often visit other countries? What were you doing in Paris?

Please wait here while your bags are x-rayed.
Please take your luggage and stand to the right.
Please open your luggage.
Please put everything on this tray.

We need to scan you with a metal detector.
You can come with us or wait until your luggage is repacked,
it will be quicker if you come with us.
Do you have any metal objects with you?

Please take off your scarf. Please take off your shirt. Please lift your arms.
Please stand with your legs apart. Please turn around and face the wall.
Lift up your foot. Lift up your other foot. Please come with me.
You may repack your bag. I will take you through the check-in.

How long have you been here? What have you been doing?
Did you meet anyone? Did anyone give you anything to carry?
Do you have any sharp objects? Please leave your bag there.
Please go with her. Please come with me.

How long have you been here? Where were you staying?
Did you meet anyone? Do you have any friends here?
Please go through this gate.
Here is your passport. Have a good flight.

'You didn't mean to let fear in'

You didn't mean to let fear in
         but she came anyway
silent with the snow that sugared the year's first hours.
You were laughing, ready for a time of ease.

She thrived on insults, a well-aimed shout,
a kick at the door. Soon she hit the jackpot.
You became afraid of going or staying,

afraid of buses, children, friends and strangers,
books and money, afraid of your teeth hurting,
your body inching towards death.

Your voice grew plaintive:
the world was cruel, there were conspiracies
on every corner, fists in the street.

As she strengthened her grip one night
and you sweated to a morning out of reach,
blood smashed against a bone anvil

and you were forged.
There was nothing magic about it.
Suddenly you were alone with a sword.

You knew she'd come again
with her lump-hammer, her leather skin.
Beating until you answered back.

# THE ROAD

In spite of all I know
I want to praise the road.
This – the A619 –
and its slalom ascent
to Wadshelf, Chander Hill,
past the refurbished Highwayman,
the lay-by where we skidded last March
as the snow blurred tarmac, field
and distant twisted spire;
this ribbon quickening
at Holymoorside.

Oil is peaking,
the internal combustion engine
wheezes its last breaths
but I love the wheel
and lean into the birch woods' yellow flecks,
the crackling flanks of beech
that might leap into life and gallop
as the road turns back
to bridleway
and track.

## WELL DRESSING

Bring eighty people working for three days.
Bring two thousand nails on a frame.
Bring ten cups of salt, a quarter-ton of clay.
Bring seven jars of poppy seeds and maize.
Bring black alder cones and coffee beans.
Bring lady's mantle and sweet cicely.
Bring hydrangea, hay and dandelion.
Bring fluorspar, coal. Bring limestone.
Bring the bent pin and the copper coin.
Bring the slub, the sock, the shirt,
the bandage, the string vest. Bring hats
and plastic bags, crutches and clouts.
Bring gold and silver. Bring a human skull.
None will put water in the empty well.

# GUILT

Guilt clicks the gate shut and squints
as her ice lolly bleeds on the path.
The hedge needs a trim. The back door
is bleached to the quick.

She's hungry to see
the dust bunnies under the bed,
the comatose mail, the rank sheets,
the life I'd have lived on the peace line

if only I'd caught the right bus.
I'd rather Jehovahs in suits.
She's no truck with chat, won't take a brew,
cuts to the chase.

I'm scared, until I remember she's ten
and the best I can do is come clean
that all I've to show for these years
is a storm-ridden desk and some pears.

# LIKE DRIVING IN FOG

Lights bloom and hurtle towards me,
fearful and grateful
to be inside a machine.

The urge to come up for air.
The pull of the road, like that night on the A1,
mile after mile of lonely heart Radio Rutland.

It could swallow a birth or a death.
Don't arrive. Don't get out.
Don't find the way in.

I'm locked to the one-by-one eyes of the A515.
Names all wiped. Monyash.
Where am I from?

Not from round here.
Not from Cubley or Hollington.
I'm from the fog.

## SNOW MIND

You won't play by the rules, pull the path
from under me, threaten fracture then vanish
when grabbed. You strangle roads with slush,
rink any thoroughfare, make me a knock-kneed
fool. But when I sweep away the deadlines
and the trudge, the muttering: *too late*, *too late*,
and look – all edges glow, the trees an infinitely
slow ballet, the only moving thing
your which-way heaven drift, your Stop and Rest.

## 3.44 A.M.

Leave your rush-hour sweat and classroom roar.
Leave your sprint towards the train door,
double-bookings, lost notes, sorry tales,
your desk pitched in its papery white grave.

For miles around you, sense collective weight
of heads on pillows, dreams' cast-lists.
Here nothing can be done. No one to phone.
Even the West Coast's on the freeway heading home.

Water slides into a glass like well-earned sleep
and as you slump across the sofa, dark takes shape,
insists you curl up, make a lap. Sink now
to purring and the deep fur of the night. Be cat.

# RETURN

I started to run,
only the barrier left –
those grumpy Leeds guards
who spring out to grab every ticket.
Though I was ready, foreseeing the men at the gate,
(but still unprepared for her smile as she leant on the wall)
all the way north I was in and out of the loo, checking my hair,
her texts in my lap and her name in my mouth, fizzing like kisses.
The past tapping away: *Are you on the right train?*
Wakefield slid by and the broken factory backs.
I reeled myself into her arms,
hand over hand.

Hand over hand
I reeled myself into her arms;
Wakefield slid by and the broken factory backs,
the past tapping away. 'R U on the right train?' –
her texts in my lap and her name in my mouth. Fizzing like kisses
all the way north, I was in and out of the loo, checking my hair,
but still unprepared for her smile as she leant on the wall,
though I was ready – foreseeing the men at the gate
who spring out to grab every ticket
(those grumpy Leeds guards).
Only the barrier left.
I started to run.